I0620368

11 CHRISTMAS SONGS FOR TTBB A CAPPELLA

JEFF BRATZ

Sign up for the HarmonyTabs email list to keep up with new
music releases, upcoming publications, and promotions:

HARMONYTABS EMAIL LIST

11 CHRISTMAS SONGS FOR TTBB A CAPPELLA
SECOND EDITION
Copyright © 2025 Jeff Bratz

To request permission, contact the publisher at publishing@HarmonyTabsMusic.com

ISBN: 978-1-961735-22-4 (paperback)
ISBN: 978-1-961735-23-1 (eBook)
ISMN: 979-0-60026-086-7 (paperback)
ISMN: 979-0-60026-087-4 (eBook)

First paperback edition October 2022

Printed in the United States of America

HarmonyTabs Music

HarmonyTabsMusic.com

CONTENTS

INTRO

First, thank you for buying this songbook. I know there are a lot of options out there and I'm honored you landed here.

I hope these songs will be as fun for you to sing through as they were for me to arrange. I've always loved the holiday season and I think that's largely due to the music that fills the air in every store, car, home, and everywhere else. I like to believe that in some small part this book will add to the spirit.

On the last page of each song is a QR code. That code will lead you to a homepage for that song where you can find additional resources including audio/video where you can hear the tune and find optional rehearsal tracks.

If at any point you have any questions, comments, suggestions, or anything else, please feel free to drop me a line: Jeff@HarmonyTabs.com.

Happy music-ing!
-Jeff

ANGELS WE HAVE HEARD ON HIGH

Traditional French Carol
Arr. Jeff Bratz

AWHHOH (TTBB)
11-11-24

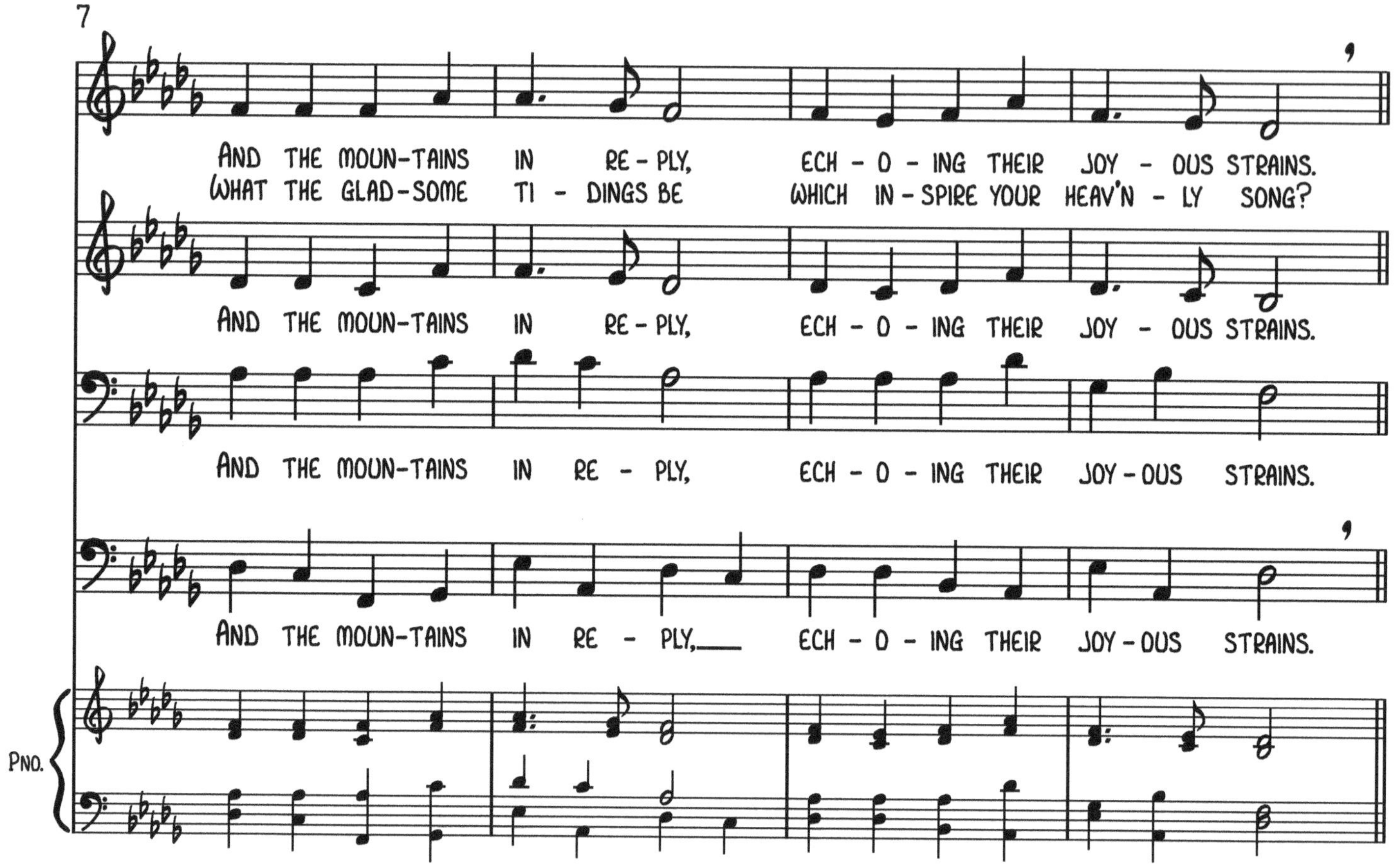
7
AND THE MOUN-TAINS IN RE - PLY, ECH - O - ING THEIR JOY - OUS STRAINS.
WHAT THE GLAD-SOME TI - DINGS BE WHICH IN - SPIRE YOUR HEAV'N - LY SONG?
AND THE MOUN-TAINS IN RE - PLY, ECH - O - ING THEIR JOY - OUS STRAINS.
AND THE MOUN-TAINS IN RE - PLY, ECH - O - ING THEIR JOY - OUS STRAINS.
AND THE MOUN-TAINS IN RE - PLY, ECH - O - ING THEIR JOY - OUS STRAINS.
PNO.

11
GLO - - - - - - - - - - -
GLO - - GLO - - GLO - -
GLO - - GLO - - GLO -
GLO GLO - GLO GLO - GLO GLO -
PNO.

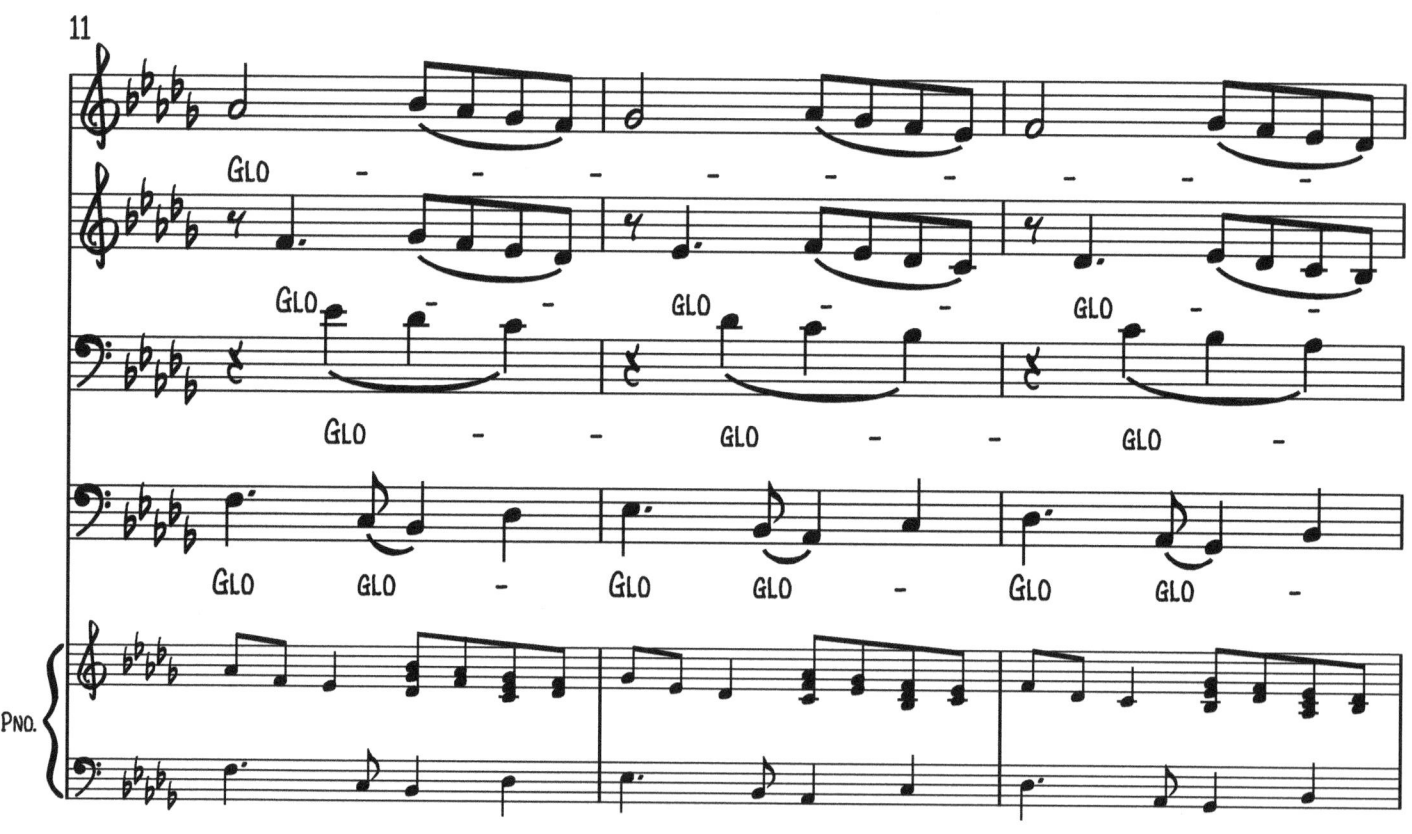

14
- RI - A , IN EX - CEL - SIS DE - O.
- RI - A , IN EX - CEL - SIS DE - O.
- RI - A IN EX - CEL - SIS DE - O.
- RI - A IN EX - CEL - SIS DE - O.
PNO.

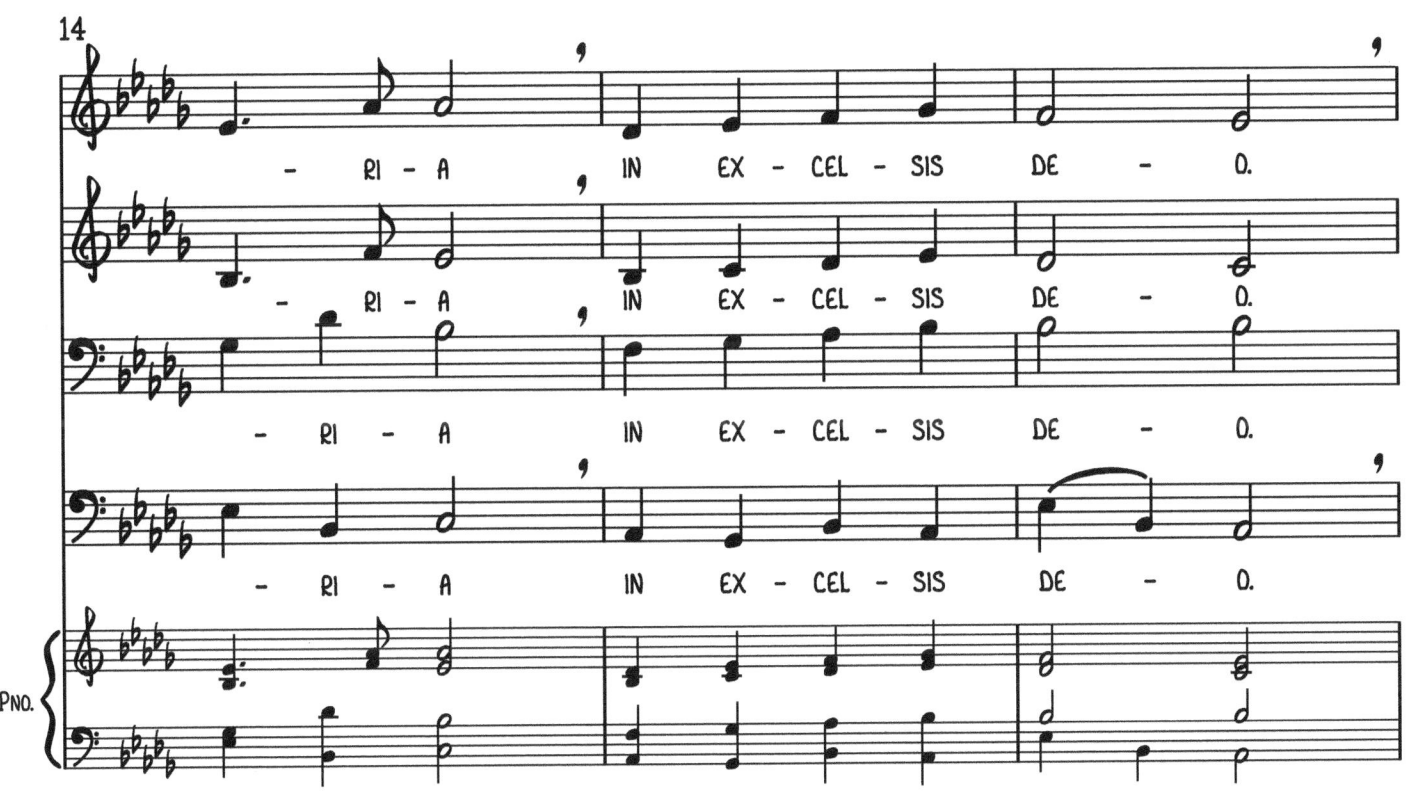

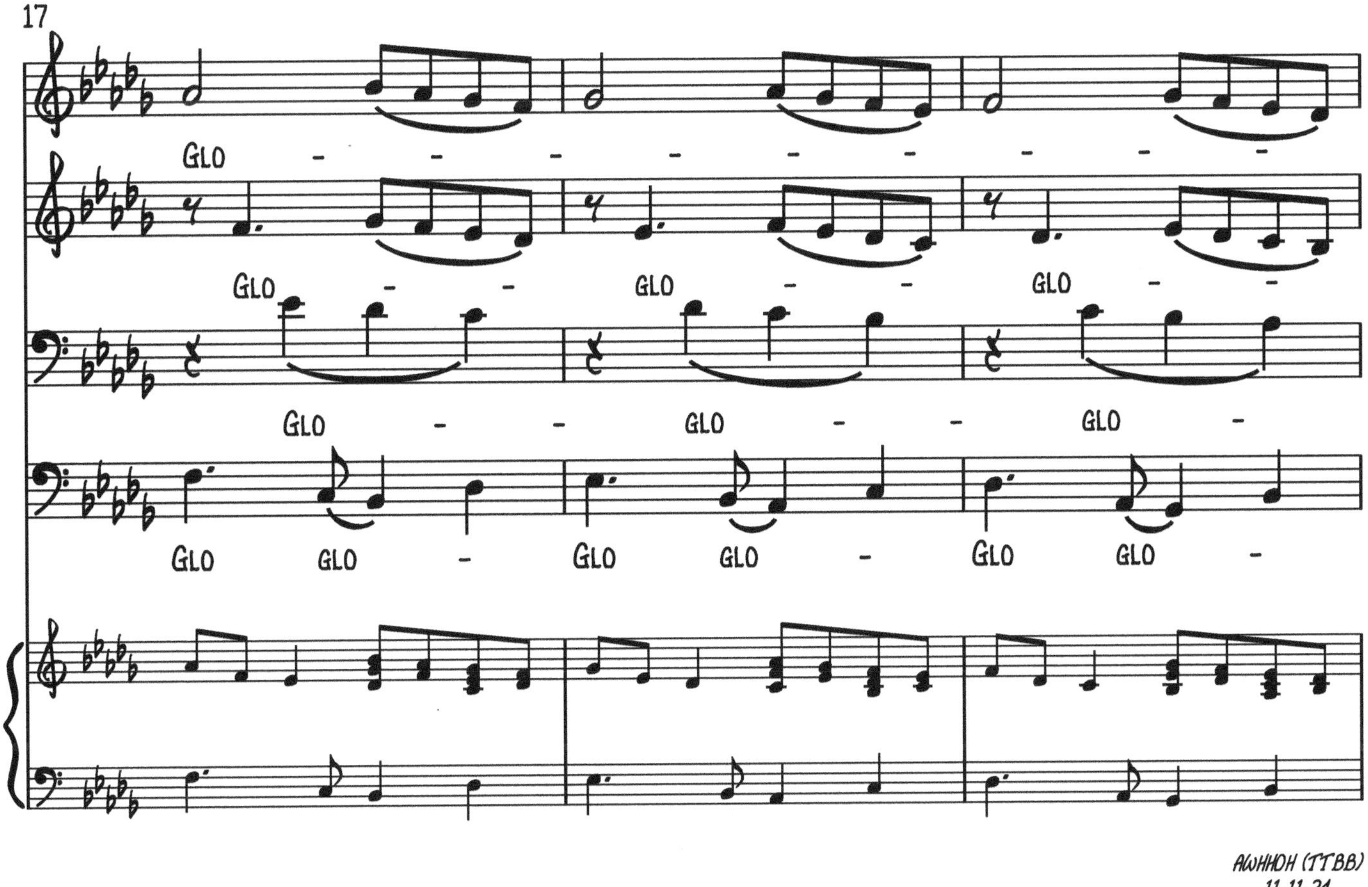
17
GLO - - - - - - - - -
GLO - - GLO - - GLO - -
GLO - - GLO - - GLO -
GLO GLO - GLO GLO - GLO GLO -
PNO.

20
1.
- RI - A , IN EX - CEL - SIS DE - - (,) O.
- RI - A , IN EX - CEL - SIS DE - - (,) O.
- RI - A , IN EX - CEL - SIS DE - - (,) O.
- RI - A IN EX - CEL - SIS DE - - O.
PNO.

24
2.
IN EX - CEL - SIS DE ,
IN EX - CEL - SIS DE - O.
IN EX - CEL - SIS DE , IN EX - CEL - SIS DE - O.
IN EX - CEL - SIS DE , IN EX - CEL - SIS DE - O.
IN EX - CEL - SIS DE - - IN EX - CEL - SIS DE - O.
PNO.

AWHHOH (TTBB)
11-11-24

Optional Additional Lyrics

(T1 solos on the second verse while the other 3 parts 'Ooh'.
If adding verses, you can choose how you'd like to split this.)

3. Come to Bethlehem and see
Him whose birth the angels sing.
Come, adore on bended knee
Christ the Lord, the newborn King.

4. See within the manger laid
Jesus, Lord of heaven and earth!
Mary, Joseph, lend your aid,
With us sing our Savior's birth.

AULD LANG SYNE

Poem by Robert Burns
Arr. Jeff Bratz

ALS (TTBB)
11-11-24

AULD LANG SYNE

AULD AC-QUAINT-ANCE BE FOR-GOT AND__ DAYS OF AULD LANG SYNE. ,FOR

AULD AC-QUAINT-ANCE BE FOR-GOT AND__ DAYS OF AULD LANG SYNE. ,FOR

AULD AC-QUAINT-ANCE BE FOR-GOT AND__ DAYS OF AULD LANG SYNE. ,FOR

Doo Doo Doo Doo Doo Doo Doo Doo FOR

AULD__ LANG__ SYNE, MY DEAR, FOR AULD__ LANG__ SYNE, WE'LL

AULD__ LANG__ SYNE, MY DEAR, FOR AULD__ LANG__ SYNE, WE'LL

AULD__ LANG__ SYNE, MY DEAR, FOR AULD__ LANG__ SYNE, ,WE'LL

AULD LANG SYNE, MY DEAR, FOR AULD__ LANG__ SYNE,__ WE'LL

ALS (TTBB)
11-11-24

AULD LANG SYNE

AWAY IN A MANGER

AIAM (TTBB)
11-15-24

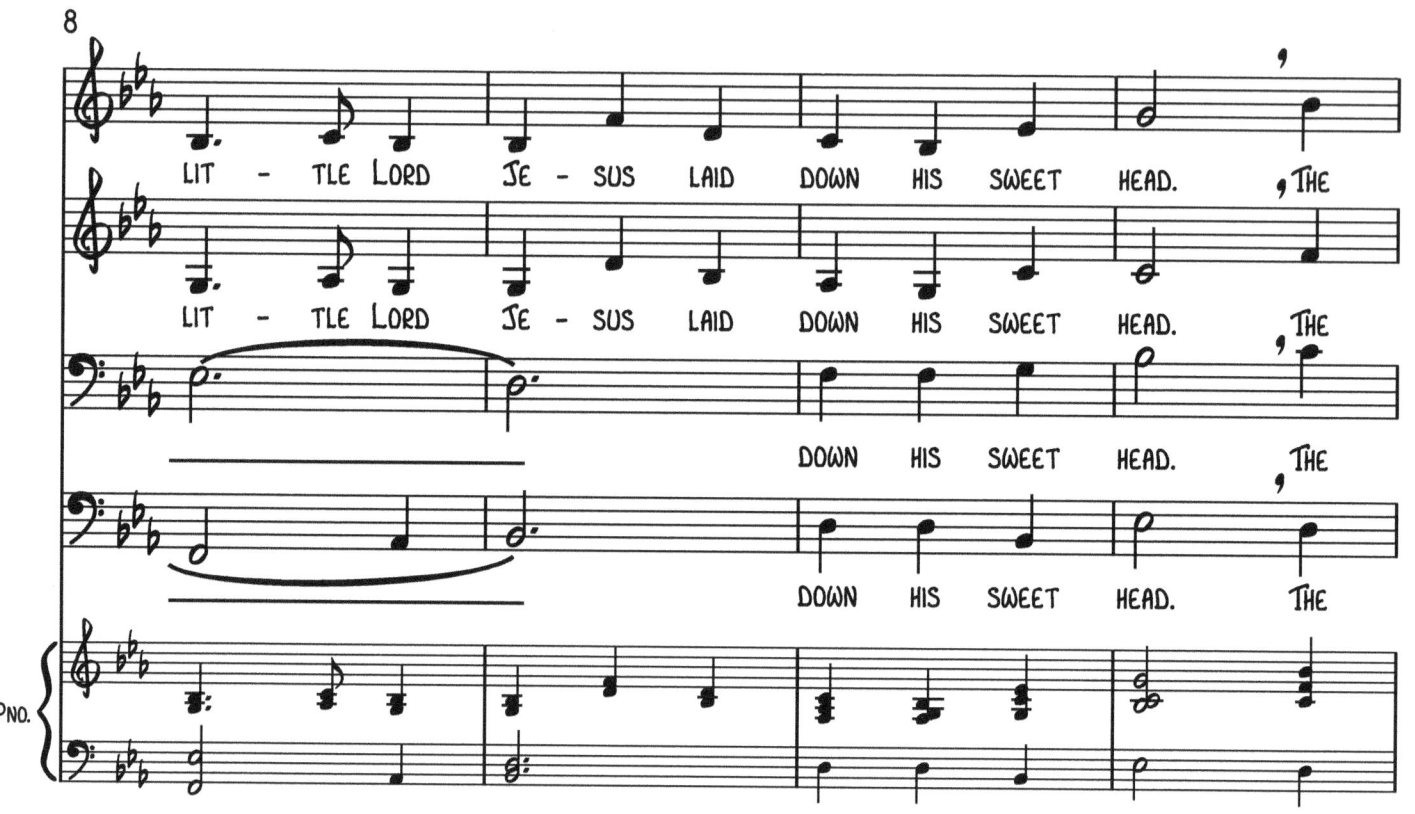

AWAY IN A MANGER

8

LIT - TLE LORD JE - SUS LAID DOWN HIS SWEET HEAD. , THE

LIT - TLE LORD JE - SUS LAID DOWN HIS SWEET HEAD. , THE

DOWN HIS SWEET HEAD. , THE

DOWN HIS SWEET HEAD. THE

Pno.

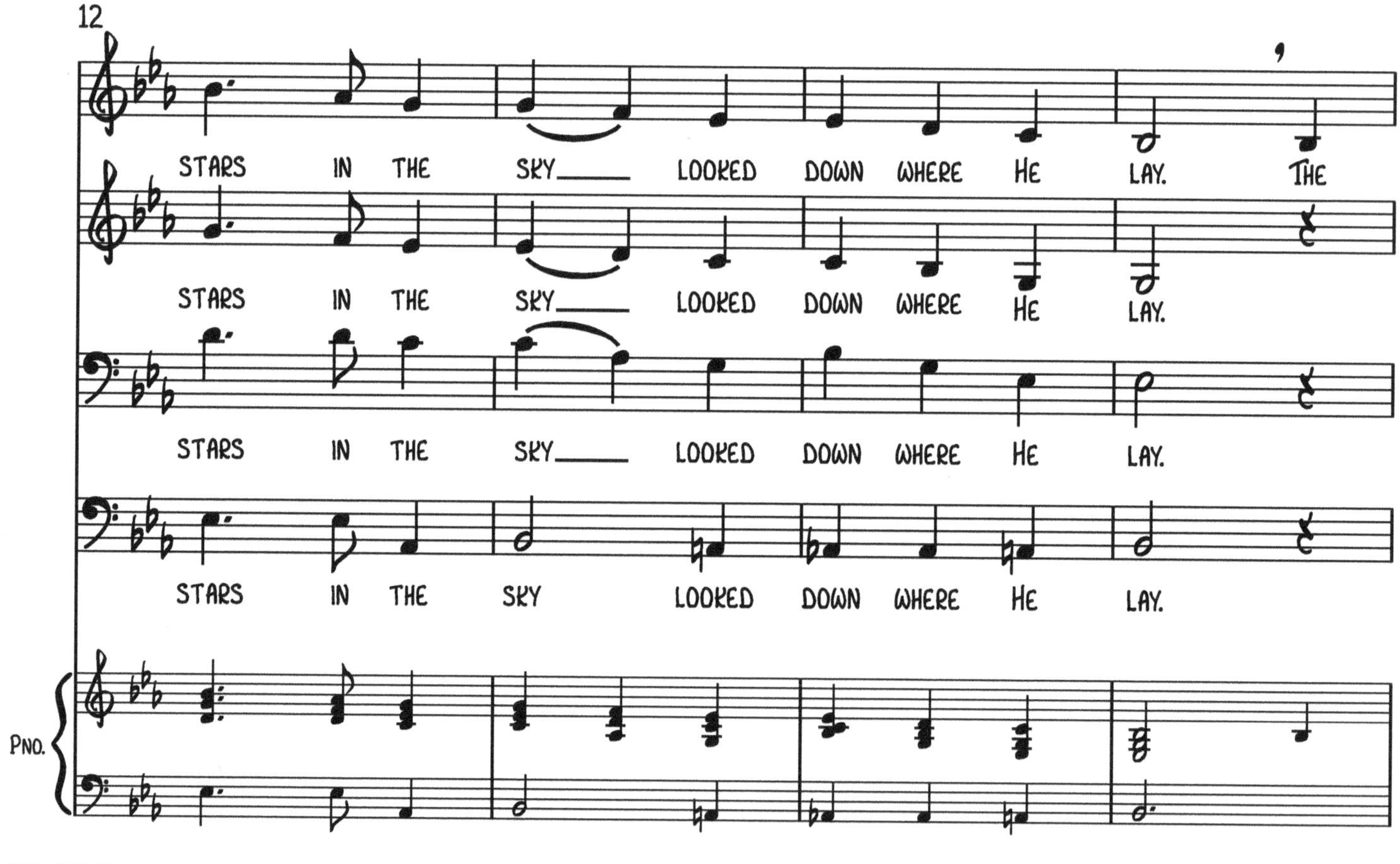

12

STARS IN THE SKY___ LOOKED DOWN WHERE HE LAY. THE

STARS IN THE SKY___ LOOKED DOWN WHERE HE LAY.

STARS IN THE SKY___ LOOKED DOWN WHERE HE LAY.

STARS IN THE SKY LOOKED DOWN WHERE HE LAY.

Pno.

AIAM (TTBB)
11-15-24

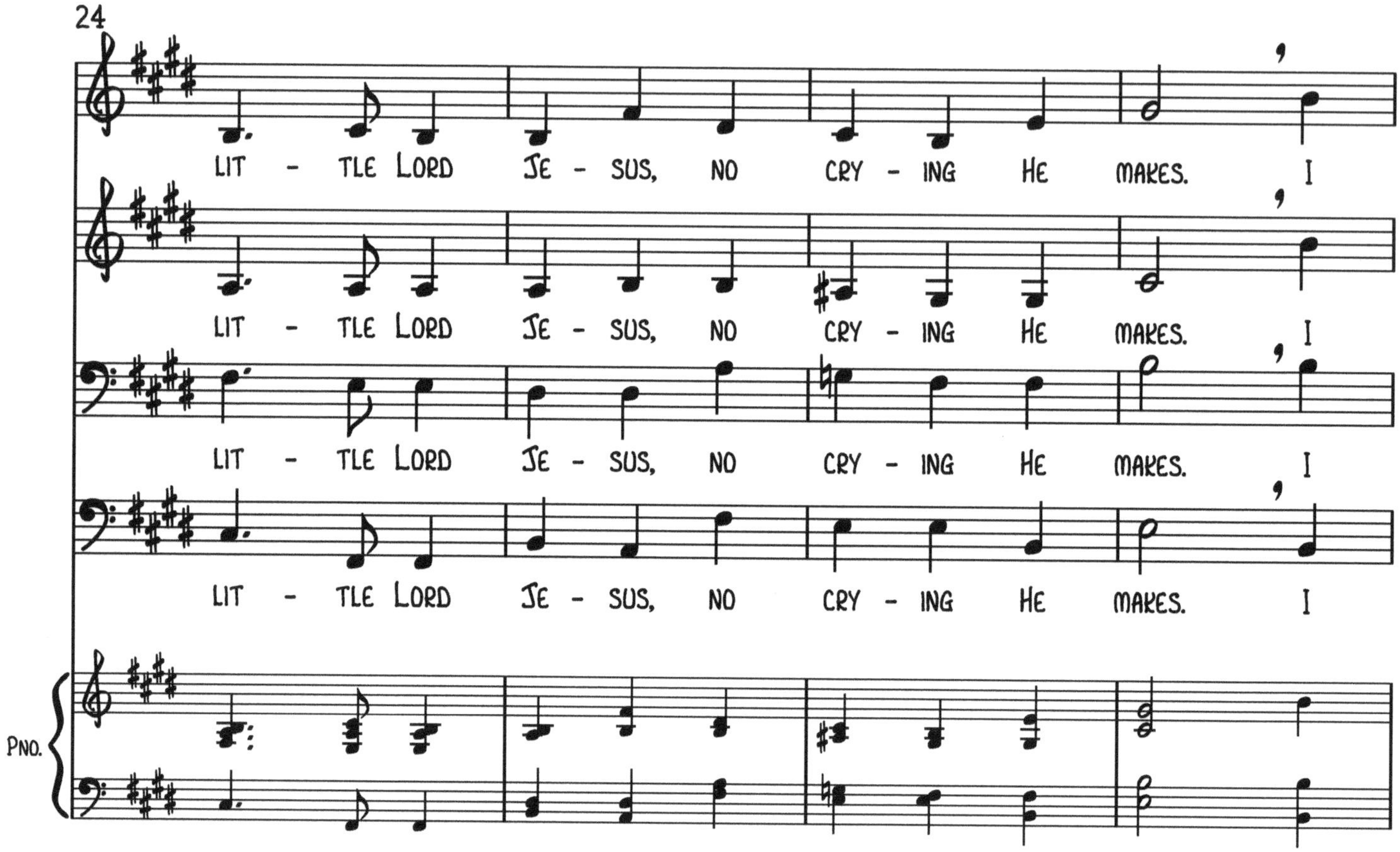
24
LIT - TLE LORD JE - SUS, NO CRY - ING HE MAKES. I
LIT - TLE LORD JE - SUS, NO CRY - ING HE MAKES. I
LIT - TLE LORD JE - SUS, NO CRY - ING HE MAKES. I
LIT - TLE LORD JE - SUS, NO CRY - ING HE MAKES. I
PNO.

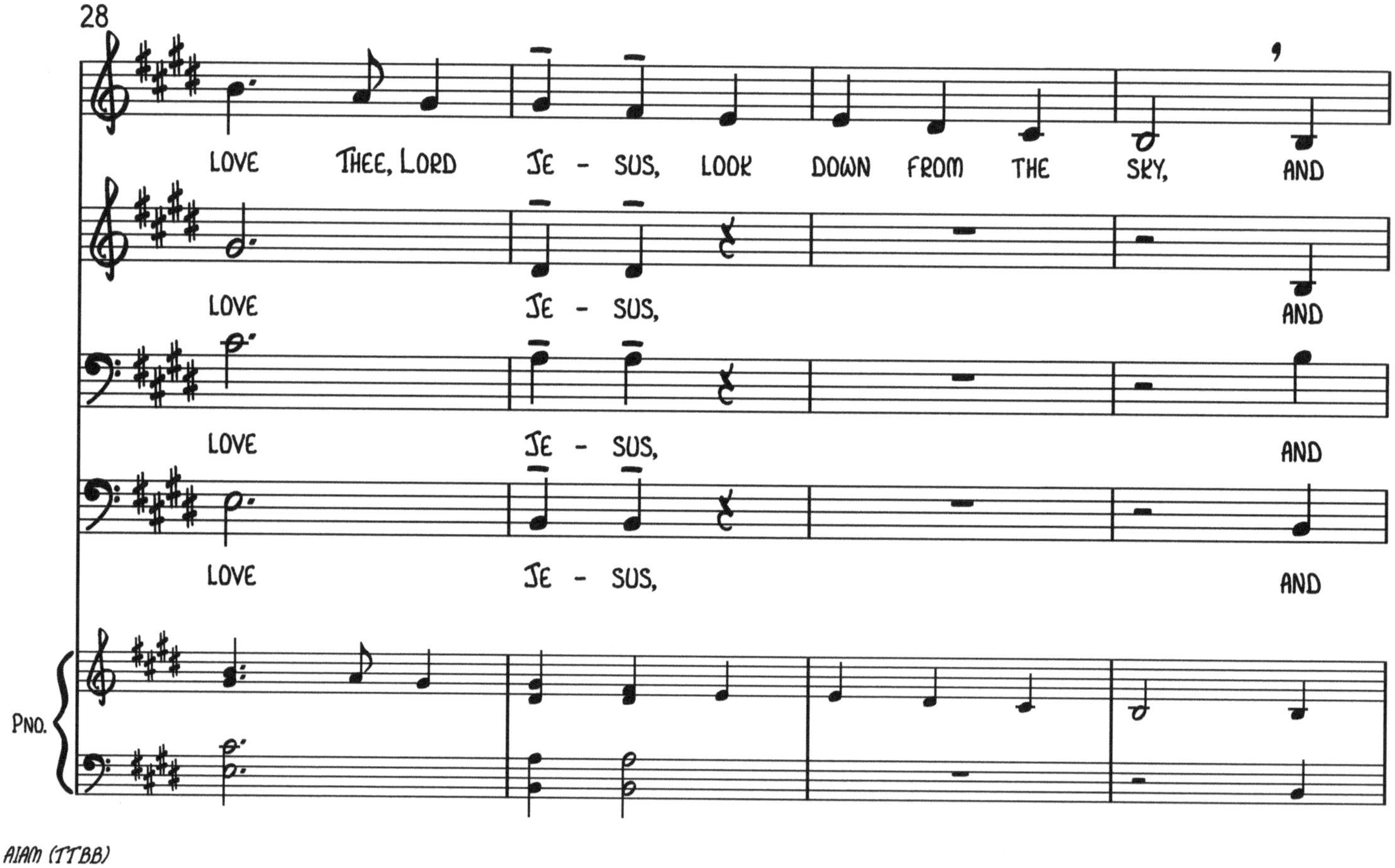
28
LOVE THEE, LORD JE - SUS, LOOK DOWN FROM THE SKY, AND
LOVE JE - SUS, AND
LOVE JE - SUS, AND
LOVE JE - SUS, AND
PNO.

AWAY IN A MANGER

AIAM (TTBB)
11-15-24

DECK THE HALLS

Traditional Welsh Carol
Arr. Jeff Bratz

DTH (TTBB)
11-17-24

DTH (TTBB)
11-17-24

DECK THE HALLS

DTH (TTBB)
11-17-24

DECK THE HALLS

DECK THE HALLS

DTH (TTBB)
11-17-24

THE FIRST NOEL

TFN (TTBB)
11-21-24

9
IN FIELDS AS THEY LAY. IN
IN FIELDS AS THEY LAY. IN
CER - TAIN POOR SHEP - HERDS IN FIELDS AS THEY LAY. IN
IN FIELDS AS THEY LAY. IN
PNO.

13
FIELDS WHERE THEY LAY KEEP - ING THEIR SHEEP, ON A
FIELDS WHERE THEY LAY KEEP - ING THEIR SHEEP, ON A
FIELDS WHERE THEY LAY KEEP - ING THEIR SHEEP, ON A
FIELDS WHERE THEY LAY KEEP - ING THEIR SHEEP, ON A
PNO.

THE FIRST NOEL

TFN (TTBB)
11-21-24

THE FIRST NOEL

TFN (TTBB)
11-21-24

THE FIRST NOEL

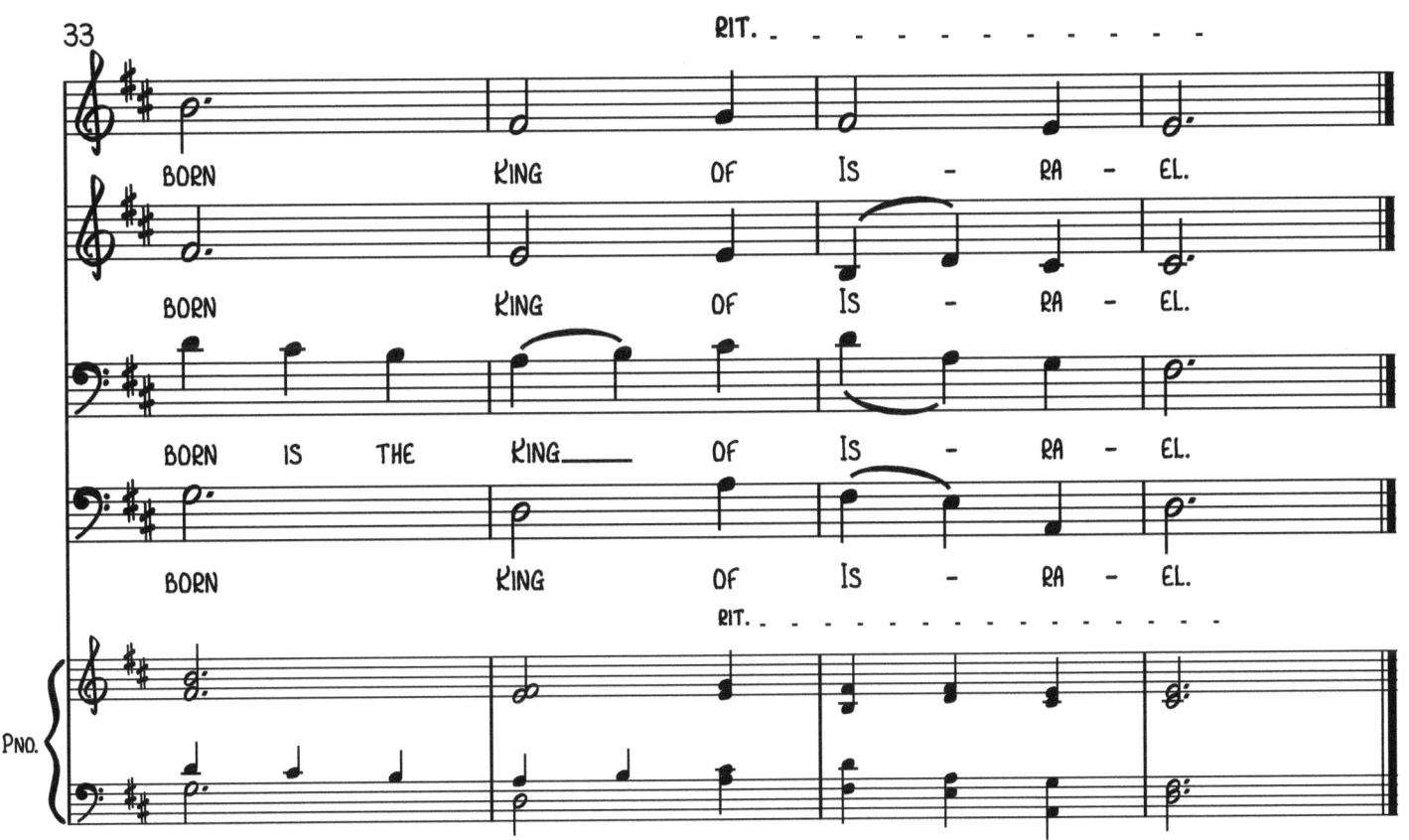

TFN (TTBB)
11-21-24

GO TELL IT ON THE MOUNTAIN

COMPILED BY
JOHN WESLEY WORK, JR.
ARR. JEFF BRATZ

GT1OTM (TTBB)
11-21-24

GO TELL IT ON THE MOUNTAIN

GT IOTM (TTBB)
11-21-24

GT1OTm (TTBB)
11-21-24

GO TELL IT ON THE MOUNTAIN

GT1OTM (TTBB)
11-21-24

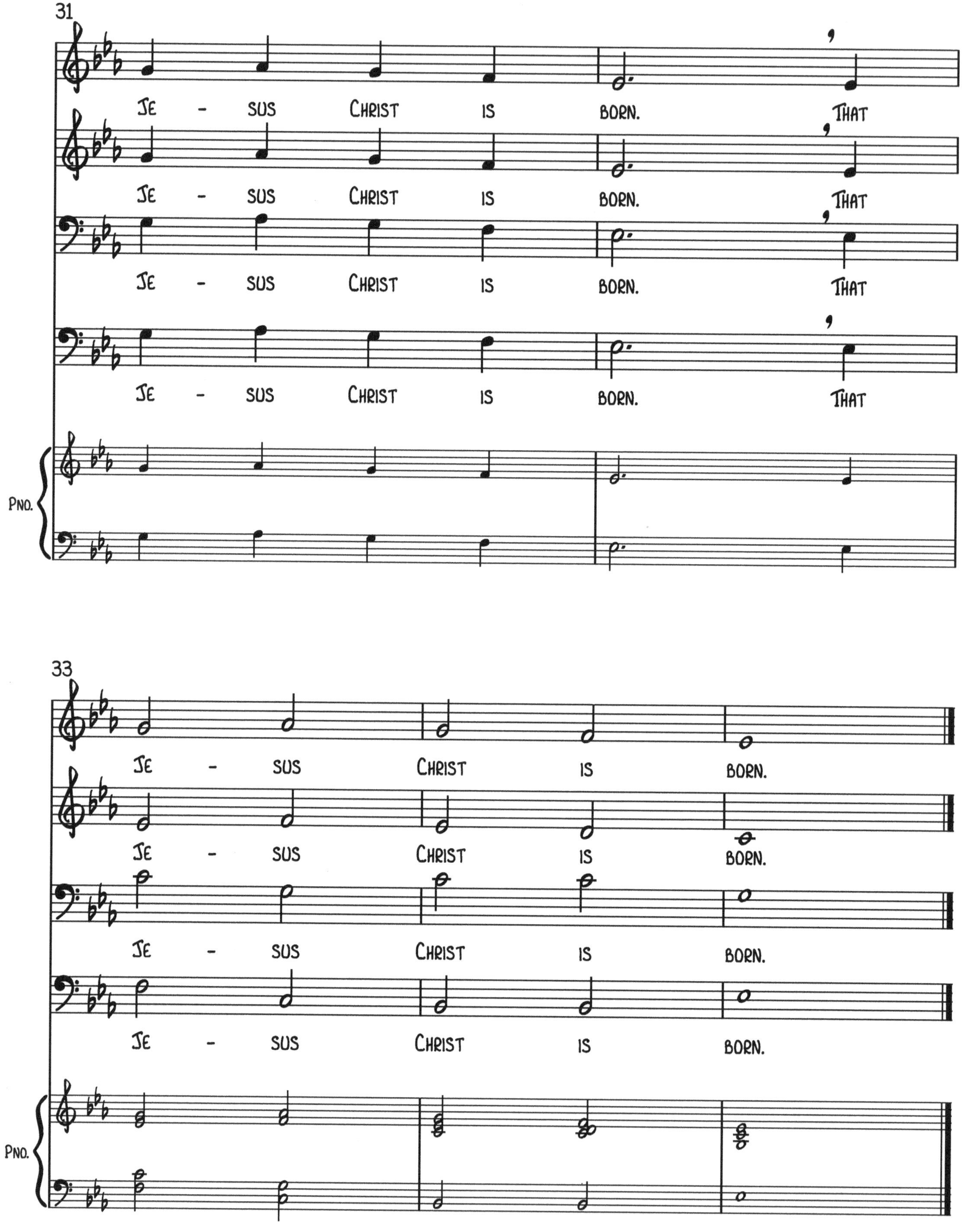
31
JE - SUS CHRIST IS BORN. THAT
JE - SUS CHRIST IS BORN. THAT
JE - SUS CHRIST IS BORN. THAT
JE - SUS CHRIST IS BORN. THAT
PNO.
33
JE - SUS CHRIST IS BORN.
JE - SUS CHRIST IS BORN.
JE - SUS CHRIST IS BORN.
JE - SUS CHRIST IS BORN.
PNO.

Additional resources for this arrangement

GOD REST YE MERRY, GENTLEMEN

19th Century English Carol
Arr. Jeff Bratz

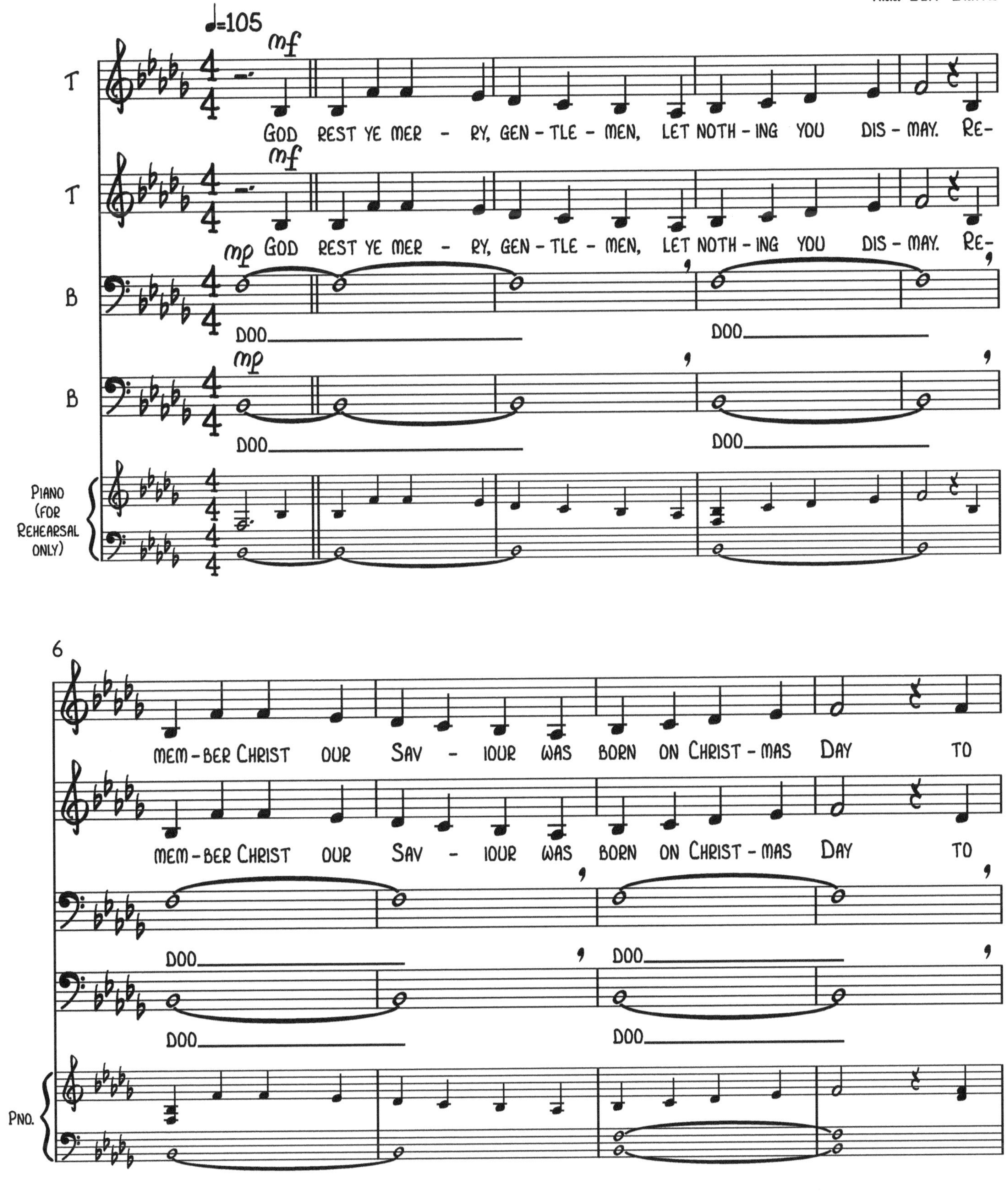

GRYMG (TTBB)
11-22-24

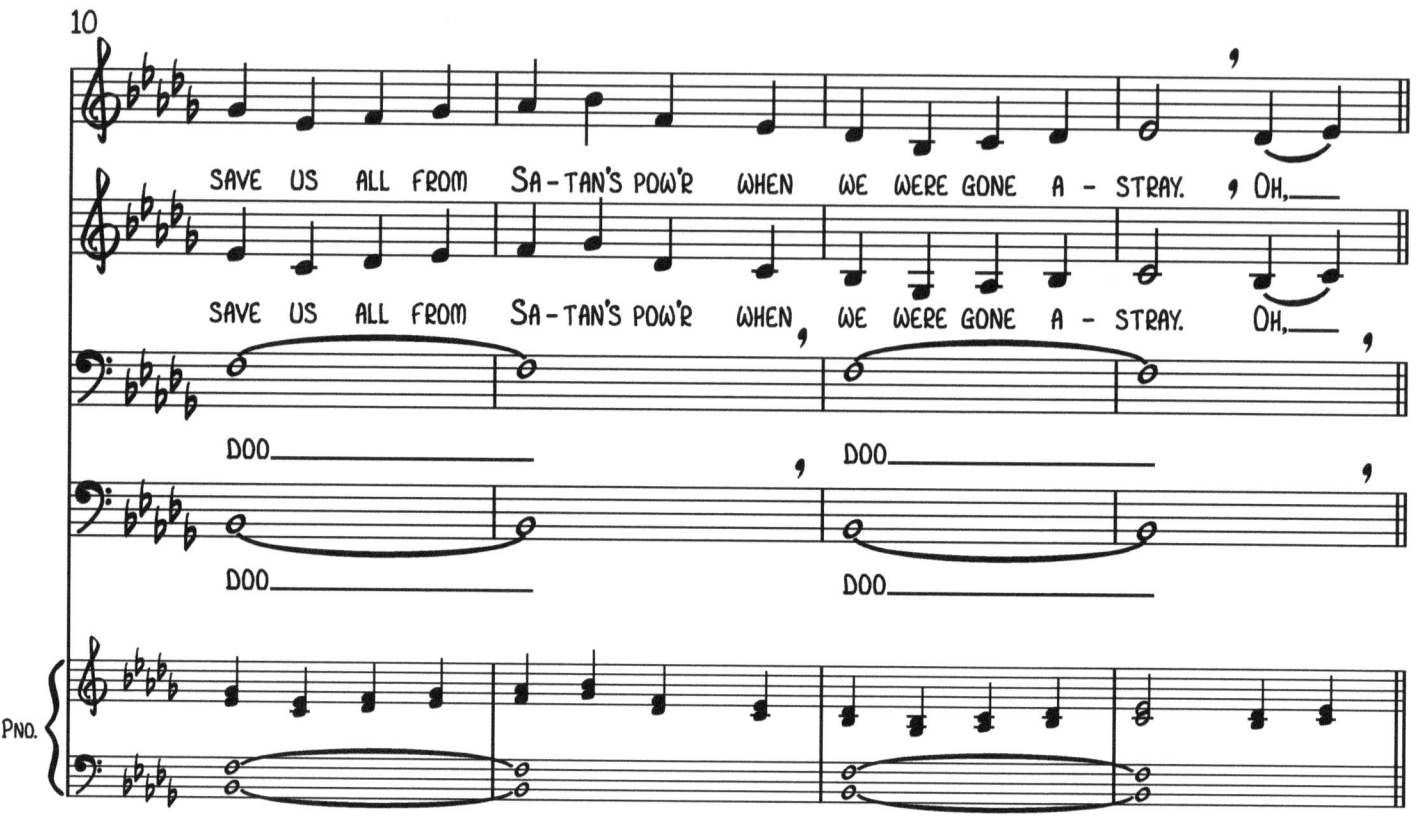

SAVE US ALL FROM SA-TAN'S POW'R WHEN WE WERE GONE A - STRAY. Oh,____

SAVE US ALL FROM SA-TAN'S POW'R WHEN WE WERE GONE A - STRAY. Oh,____

DOO_____ DOO_____

DOO_____ DOO_____

TI - DINGS OF COM - FORT AND JOY, COM-FORT AND JOY. Oh,____

TI - DINGS OF COM - FORT AND JOY, COM-FORT AND JOY. Oh,____

DOO_____ DOO_____

DOO_____ DOO_____

GRYMG (TTBB)
11-22-24

- 32 -

GOD REST YE MERRY, GENTLEMEN

GRYMG (TTBB)
11-22-24

GOD REST YE MERRY, GENTLEMEN

Lyrics (Tenor/Bass voices, measures 26–29):

UN-TO CER-TAIN SHEP-HERDS, BROUGHT TI-DINGS OF THE SAME, HOW

BLESS-ED AN-GEL CAME, AND UN-TO CER-TAIN SHEP-HERDS, BROUGHT

CAME, AND UN-TO CER-TAIN SHEP-HERDS, BROUGHT TI-DINGS OF THE

FA-THER A BLESS-ED AN-GEL CAME, AND UN-TO CER-TAIN

Lyrics (measures 30–33):

THAT IN BETH-LE-HEM WAS BORN THE SON OF GOD BY NAME. Oh,___

TI-DINGS OF THE SAME, THE SON OF GOD BY NAME.___ Oh,

SAME, IN BETH-LE-HEM THE SON OF GOD BY NAME. Oh,___

SHEP-HERDS, BROUGHT TI-DINGS OF THE SON OF GOD BY NAME. Oh,

GOD REST YE MERRY, GENTLEMEN

GRYMG (TTBB)
11-22-24

GOD REST YE MERRY, GENTLEMEN

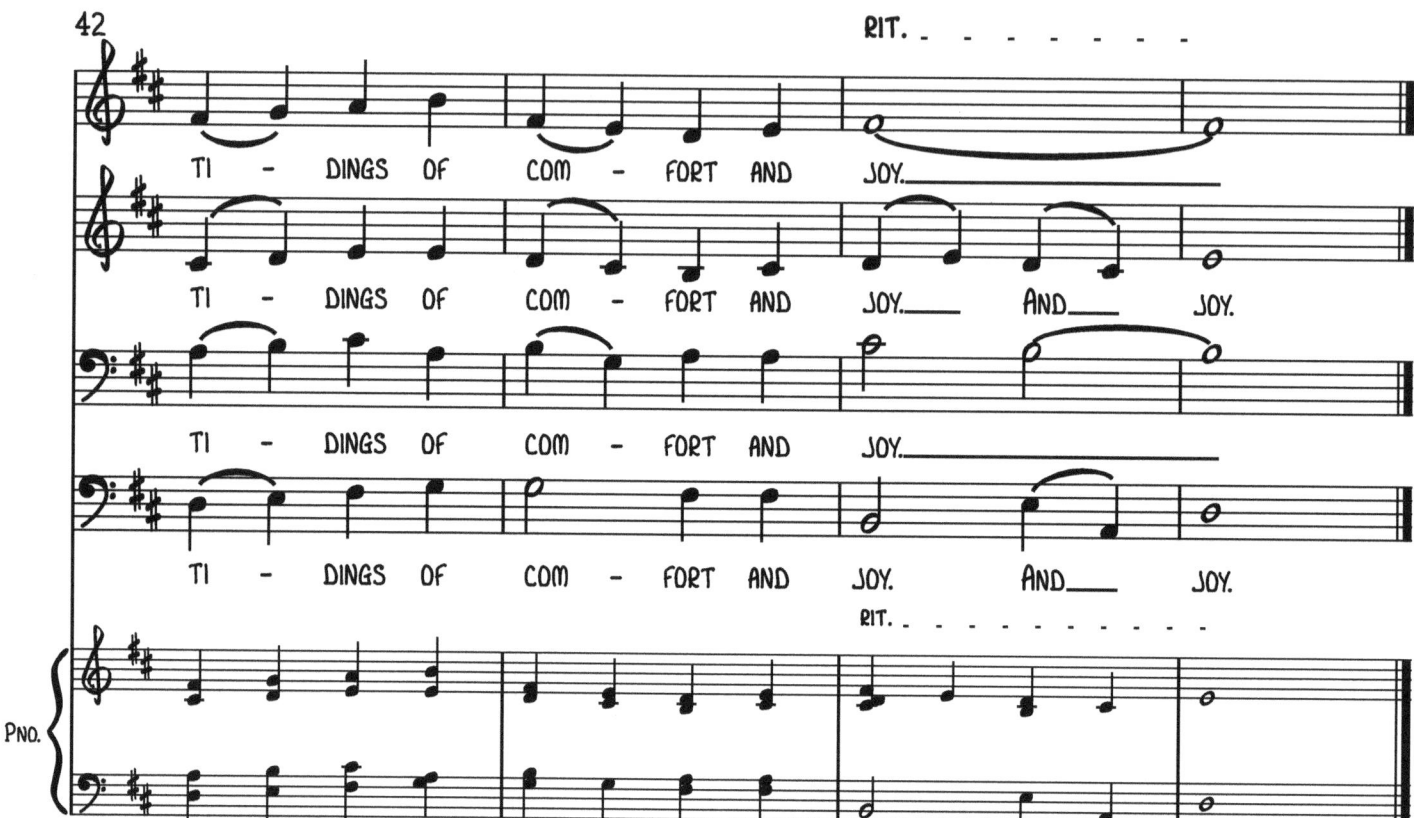

GRYMG (TTBB)
11-22-24

HALLELUJAH CHORUS
(ABRIDGED)

George Friedrich Handel
arr. Jeff Bratz

HC (TTBB)
12-5-24

HALLELUJAH CHORUS (ABRIDGED)

HC (TTBB)
12-5-24

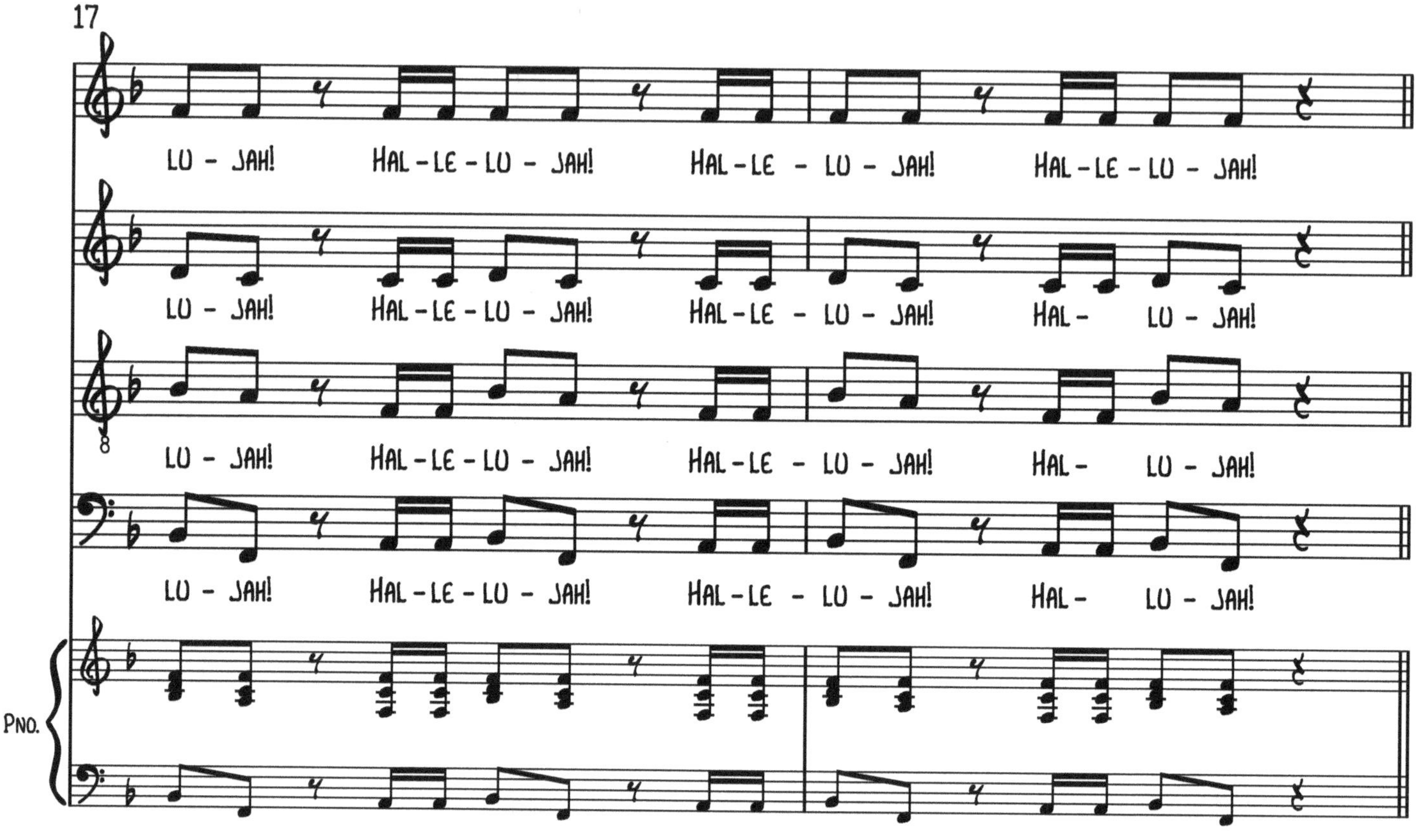
17
LU - JAH! HAL - LE - LU - JAH! HAL - LE - LU - JAH! HAL - LE - LU - JAH!
LU - JAH! HAL - LE - LU - JAH! HAL - LE - LU - JAH! HAL- LU - JAH!
LU - JAH! HAL - LE - LU - JAH! HAL - LE - LU - JAH! HAL- LU - JAH!
LU - JAH! HAL - LE - LU - JAH! HAL - LE - LU - JAH! HAL- LU - JAH!
PNO.

19
f
AND HE SHALL REIGN FOR
f
mf
AND HE SHALL REIGN FOR - EV - ER AND EV - ER, FOR EV - ER AND
PNO.

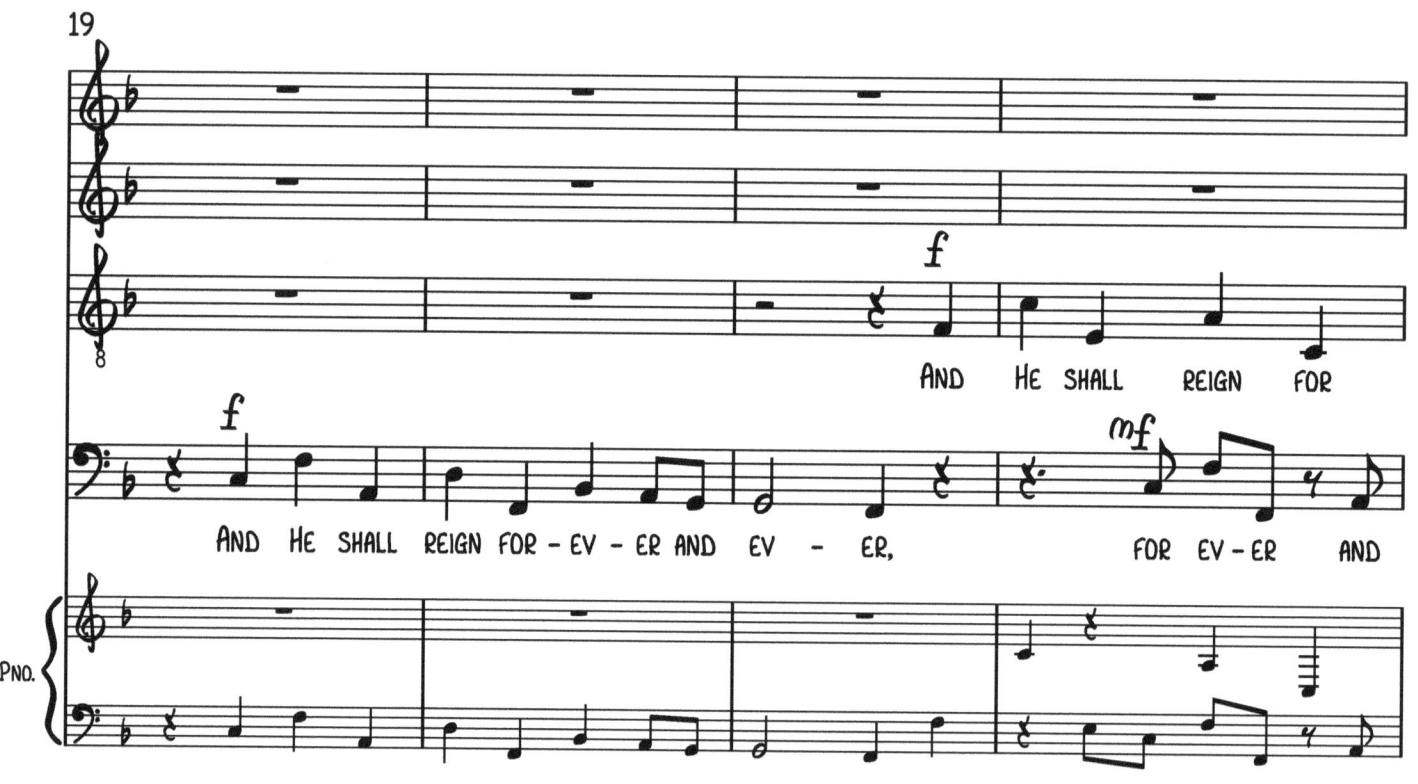

HALLELUJAH CHORUS (ABRIDGED)

HC (TTBB)
12-5-24

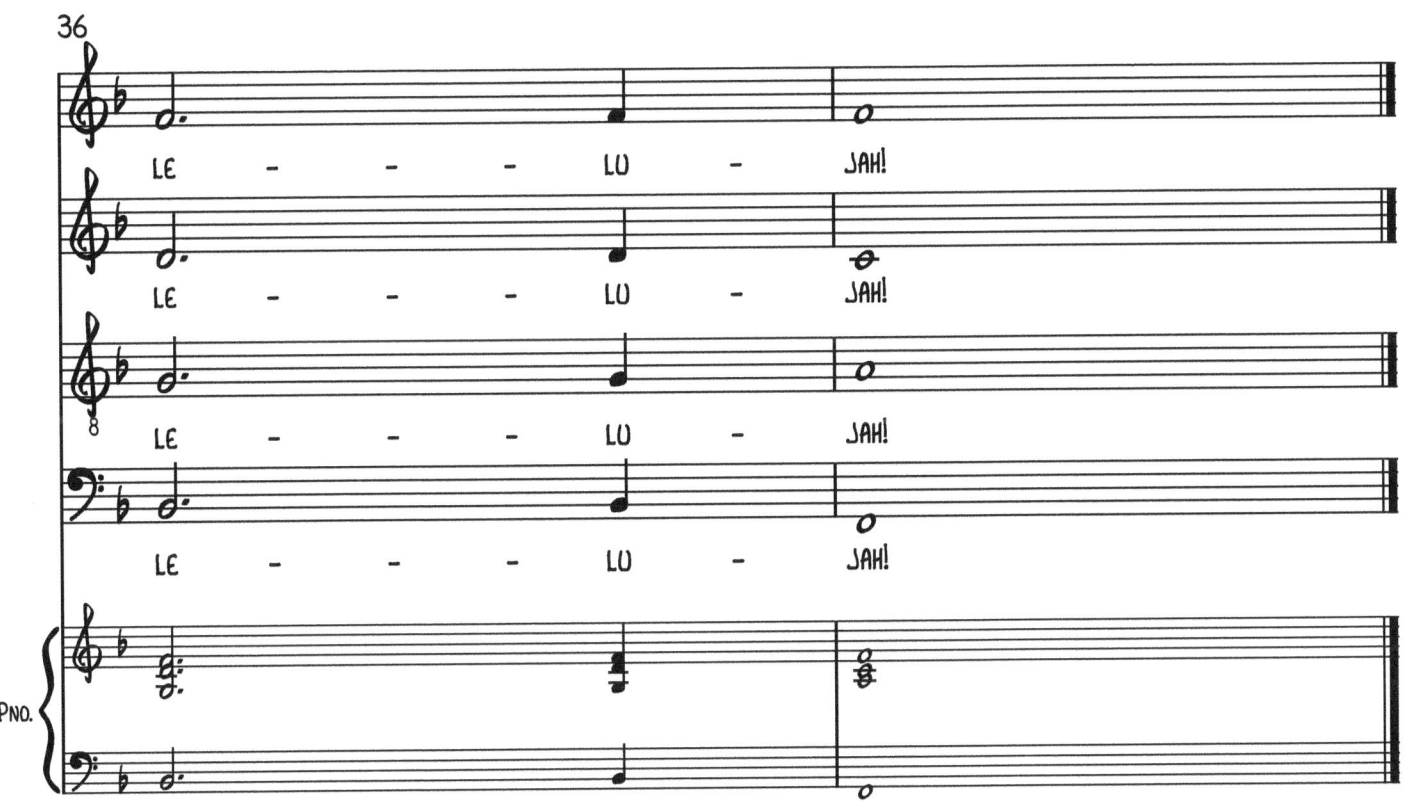

HC (TTBB)
12-5-24

HARK! THE HERALD ANGELS SING

Felix Mendelssohn
Lyrics by Charles Wesley
and George Whitefield
Arr. Jeff Bratz

HTHAS (TTBB)
12-16-24

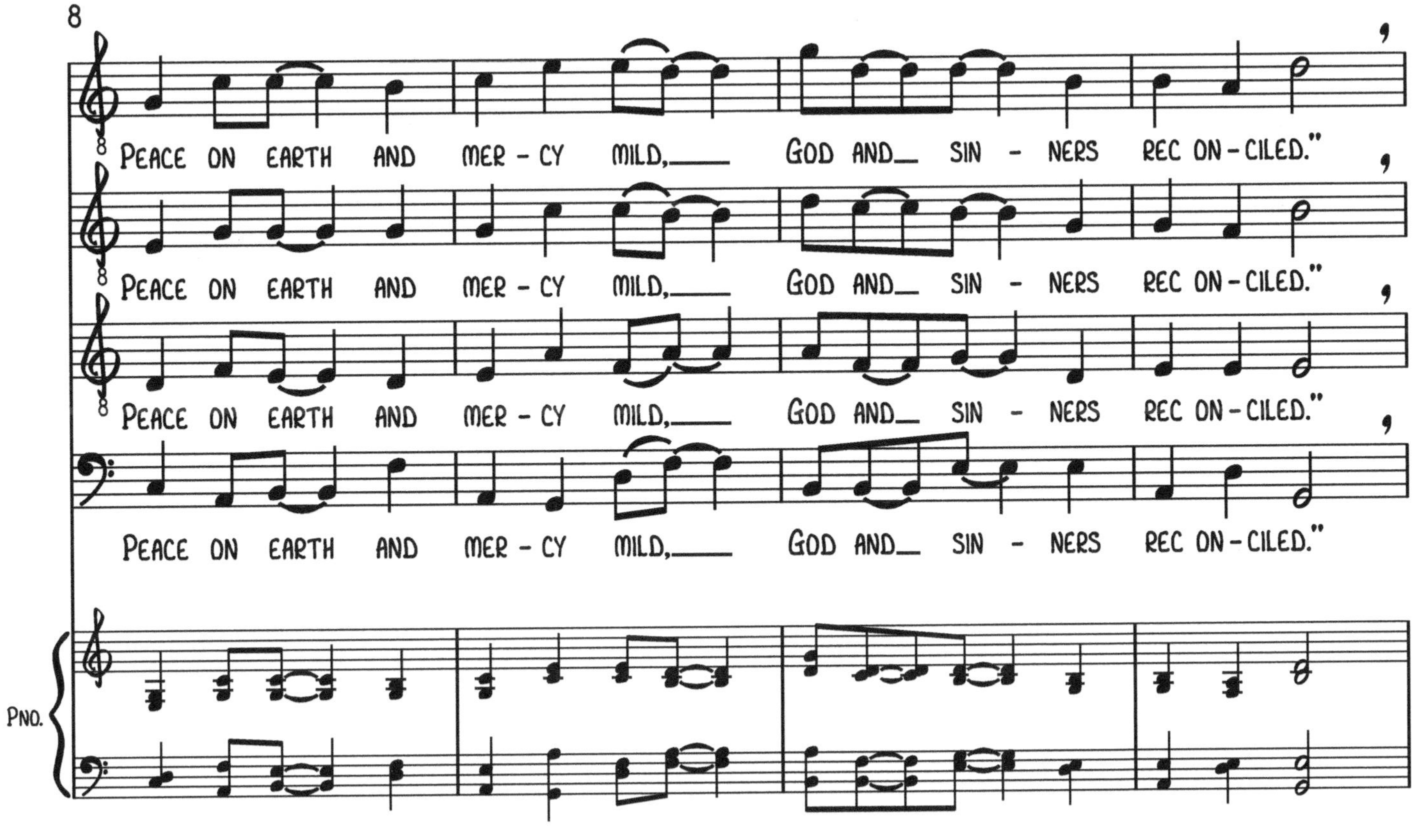
8
PEACE ON EARTH AND MER - CY MILD,___ GOD AND___ SIN - NERS REC ON - CILED."
PEACE ON EARTH AND MER - CY MILD,___ GOD AND___ SIN - NERS REC ON - CILED."
PEACE ON EARTH AND MER - CY MILD,___ GOD AND___ SIN - NERS REC ON - CILED."
PEACE ON EARTH AND MER - CY MILD,___ GOD AND___ SIN - NERS REC ON - CILED."
PNO.

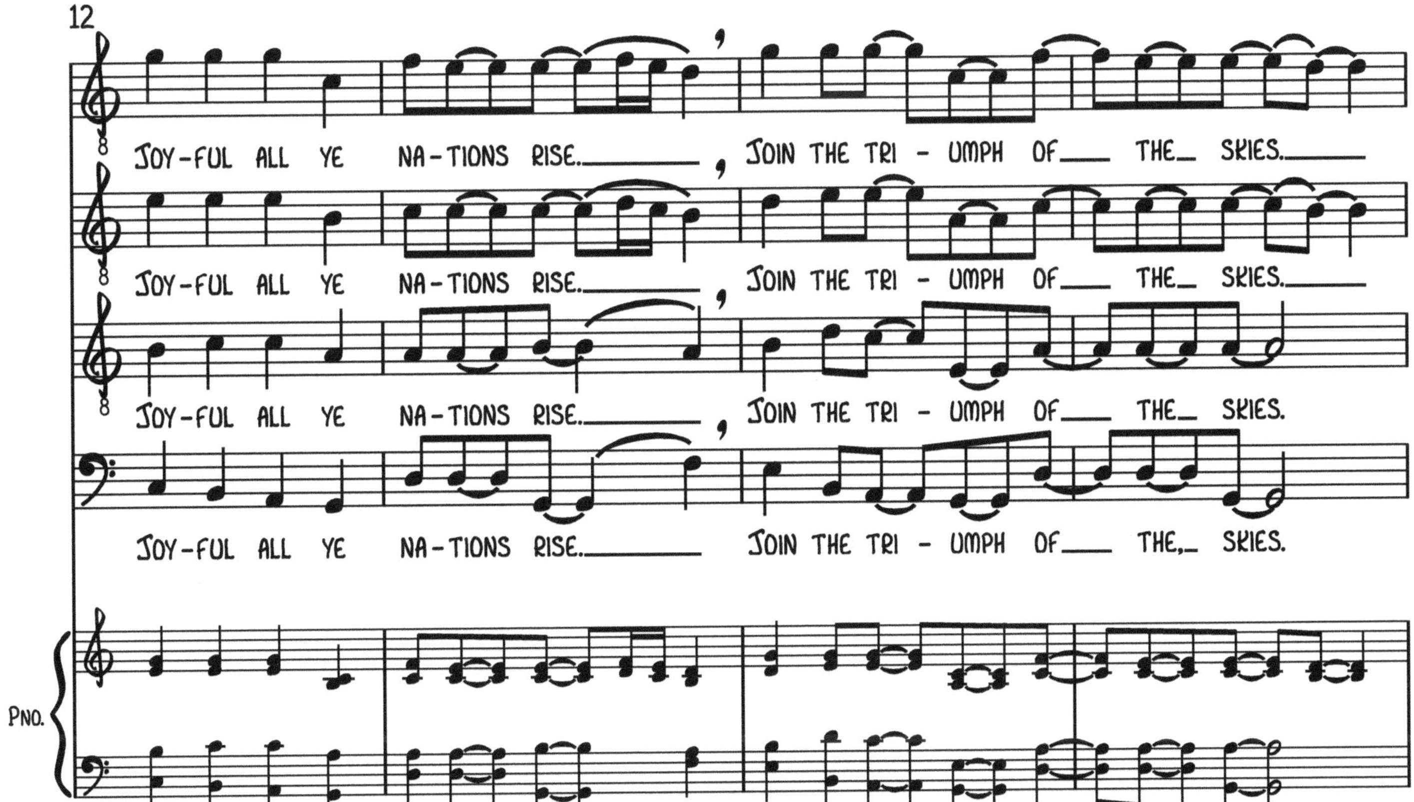
12
JOY - FUL ALL YE NA - TIONS RISE.______, JOIN THE TRI - UMPH OF___ THE___ SKIES.______
JOY - FUL ALL YE NA - TIONS RISE.______, JOIN THE TRI - UMPH OF___ THE___ SKIES.______
JOY - FUL ALL YE NA - TIONS RISE.______, JOIN THE TRI - UMPH OF___ THE___ SKIES.
JOY - FUL ALL YE NA - TIONS RISE.______ JOIN THE TRI - UMPH OF___ THE,___ SKIES.
PNO.

16

WITH AN-GEL-IC___ HOST___ PRO - CLAIM, "CHRIST IS___ BORN IN BETH-LE - HEM."

WITH AN-GEL-IC___ HOST___ PRO - CLAIM, "CHRIST IS___ BORN IN BETH-LE - HEM."

WITH AN-GEL-IC___ HOST___ PRO - CLAIM, "CHRIST IS___ BORN IN BETH-LE - HEM."

WITH AN-GEL-IC___ HOST___ PRO - CLAIM, "CHRIST IS___ BORN IN BETH-LE - HEM."

Pno.

20

HARK! THE HER-ALD AN-GELS SING, "GLO - RY___ TO THE NEW - BORN KING!"___ HAIL,

HARK! THE HER-ALD AN-GELS SING, "GLO - RY___ TO THE NEW - BORN KING!"___ HAIL,

HARK! THE HER-ALD AN-GELS SING, "GLO - RY___ TO THE NEW - BORN KING!"___ HAIL,

HARK! THE HER-ALD AN-GELS SING, "GLO - RY TO THE NEW - BORN KING!"___ HAIL,

Pno.

HTHAS (TTBB)
12-16-24

HTHAS (TTBB)
12-16-24

32

(Vocal parts — lyrics:)

MILD HE LAYS HIS GLO-RY__ BY,_____ BORN THAT MAN_ NO__ MORE__ MAY_ DIE._____

MILD HE LAYS HIS GLO-RY__ BY,_____ BORN THAT MAN_ NO__ MORE__ MAY_ DIE.

MILD HE LAYS HIS GLO-RY__ BY,_____ BORN THAT MAN_ NO__ MORE__ MAY_ DIE._____

MILD HE LAYS HIS GLO-RY__ BY, BORN THAT MAN_ NO__ MORE__ MAY_ DIE._

Pno.

36

BORN TO RAISE THE_ SONG__ OF__ EARTH, BORN TO__ GIVE THEM SEC-OND BIRTH.

BORN TO RAISE THE_ SONG__ OF__ EARTH, BORN TO__ GIVE THEM SEC-OND BIRTH.

BORN TO RAISE THE_ SONG__ OF__ EARTH, BORN TO__ GIVE THEM SEC-OND BIRTH.

BORN TO RAISE THE_ SONG__ OF__ EARTH, BORN TO GIVE THEM SEC-OND BIRTH.

Pno.

HARK! THE HERALD ANGELS SING

HTHAS (TTBB)
12-16-24

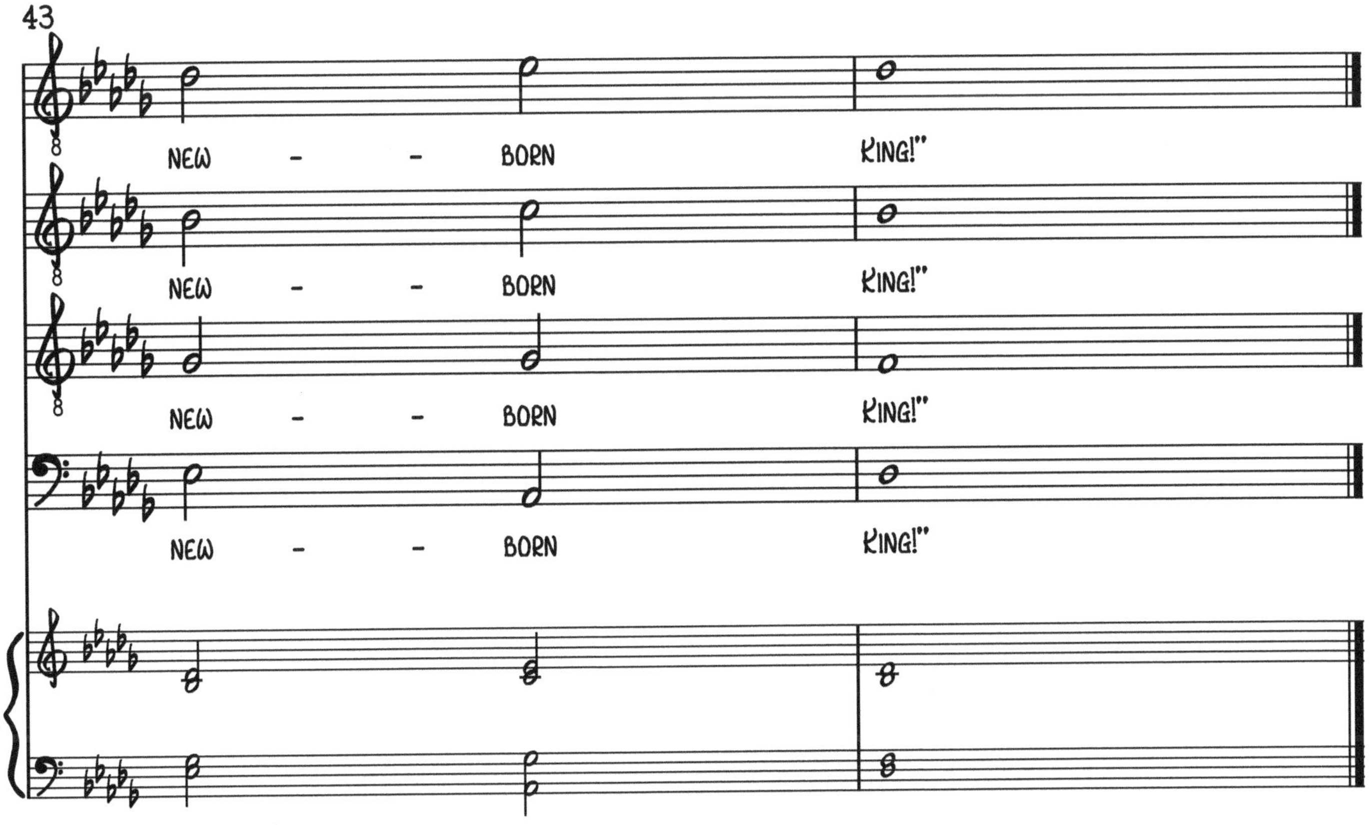

I SAW THREE SHIPS

Traditional
Arr. Jeff Bratz

ISTS (TTBB)
12-17-24

7

mf

DOON

PRAY,

SAW THREE SHIPS COME SAIL - ING IN ON CHRIST-MAS DAY IN THE MORN - ING. PRAY,

DOON

DOON

PNO.

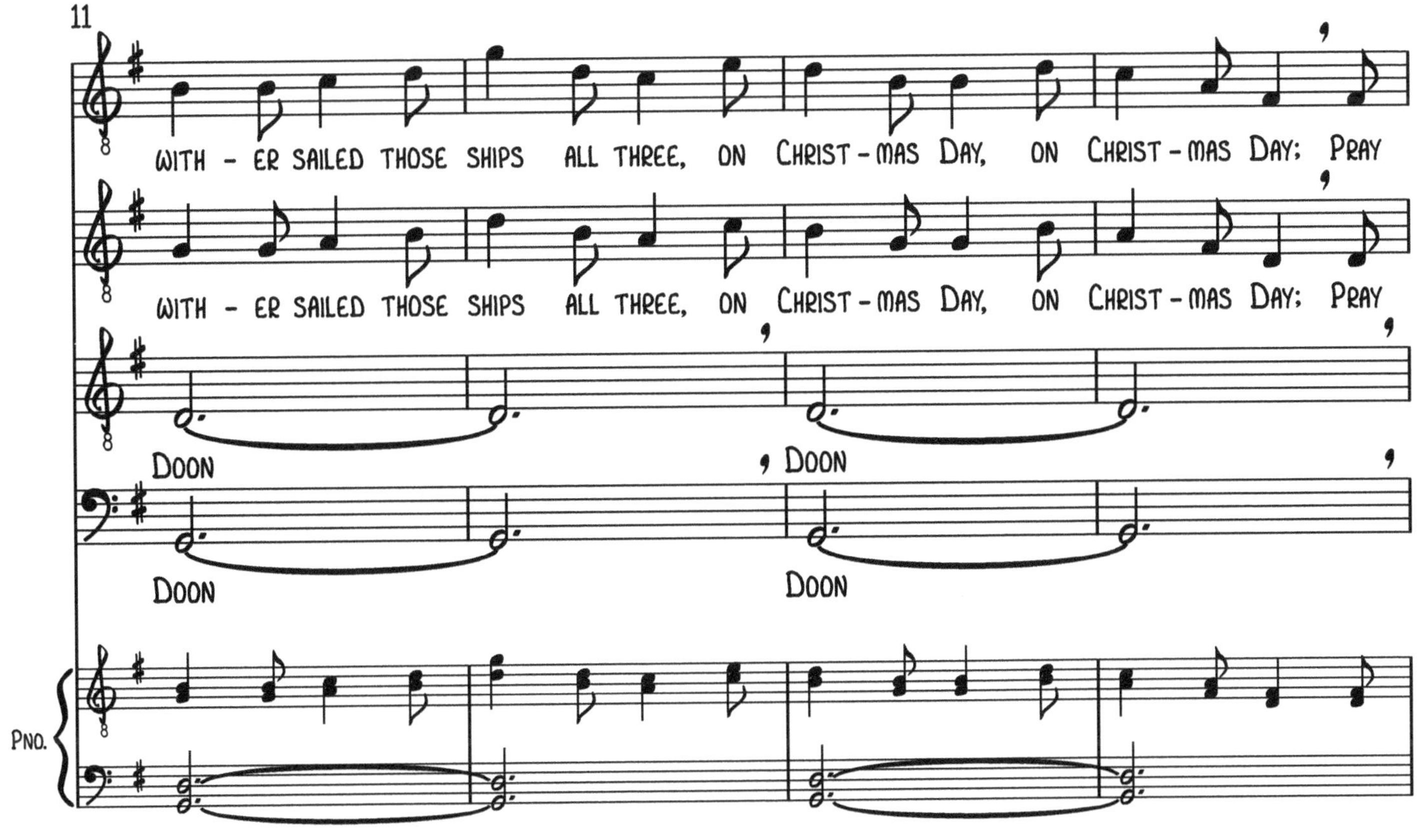

11

WITH - ER SAILED THOSE SHIPS ALL THREE, ON CHRIST - MAS DAY, ON CHRIST - MAS DAY; PRAY

WITH - ER SAILED THOSE SHIPS ALL THREE, ON CHRIST - MAS DAY, ON CHRIST - MAS DAY; PRAY

DOON , DOON

DOON DOON

PNO.

ISTS (TTBB)
12-17-24

15

WITH — ER SAILED THOSE SHIPS ALL THREE, ON CHRIST-MAS DAY IN THE MORN — ING?

WITH — ER SAILED THOSE SHIPS ALL THREE, ON CHRIST-MAS DAY IN THE MORN — ING?

DOON   DOON   mf

DOON   DOON   DOON

Pno.

19

THEY SAILED IN — TO BETH — LE-HEM ON CHRIST-MAS DAY, ON CHRIST-MAS DAY;

THEY SAILED IN — TO BETH — LE-HEM ON CHRIST-MAS DAY, ON CHRIST-MAS DAY;

mf

THEY SAILED IN — TO BETH — LE-HEM ON CHRIST-MAS DAY, ON CHRIST-MAS DAY;

DOON   DOON   DOON   DOON   DOON

Pno.

I SAW THREE SHIPS

ISTS (TTBB)
12-17-24

I SAW THREE SHIPS

I SAW THREE SHIPS

- 55 -

ISTS (TTBB)
12-17-24

I SAW THREE SHIPS

ISTS (TTBB)
12-17-24

THE TWELVE-ISH DAYS OF CHRISTMAS

TTDOC (TTBB)
1-1-25

THE TWELVE-ISH DAYS OF CHRISTMAS

TTDOC (TTBB)
1-1-25

THE TWELVE-ISH DAYS OF CHRISTMAS

TTDOC (TTBB)
1-1-25

THE TWELVE-ISH DAYS OF CHRISTMAS

TTDOC (TTBB)
1-1-25

THE TWELVE-ISH DAYS OF CHRISTMAS

* STAY IN TIME, BUT FEEL FREE TO PLAY WITH THE WORDS *

EX. PEEL OFF EARLY ONE BY ONE TO COMPLAIN ABOUT ALL
THE GIFTS, THEN PEEL OFF THE BASS AS A VOICE OF REASON.
HAVE THE HIGH TENOR HAPPILY CONTINUE THE LYRICS ALL THE
WAY. BUT ALL SILENT ON BEAT 4 AFTER 'SIX GEESE A-LAYING'.

TWELVE DRUMMERS DRUMMING,
'LEVEN PIPERS PIPING,
TEN LORDS A-LEAPING,
NINE LADIES DANCING,
EIGHT MAIDS A-MILKING,
SEVEN SWANS A-SWIMMING,

TTDOC (TTBB)
1-1-25

FINAL WORDS

Please consider leaving a review of this book. I would greatly appreciate it. It will help me to continue on this book writing journey I've set off on.

Thank you in advance!

LEAVE A REVIEW

HARMONYTABS EMAIL LIST

Once again, here is the link to the HarmonyTabs email list to keep you up to speed on any new music, publications, and promotions.

ABOUT THE AUTHOR

Jeff Bratz has a degree in Professional Music from the School for Music Vocations and a Professional Certificate in Music Theory and Composition from Berklee College of Music. He's a composer and arranger specializing in vocal arrangements. In a former life, Jeff was a music teacher for grades pre-k through high school. He has sung in dozens of vocal groups including The Dickens Carolers at Disneyland's *Club 33*, The Fault Line on *America's Got Talent*, and Manhattan Transfer tribute group LA Transfer. He was also part of the Downbeat award-winning First Take. He currently performs with rock band RaDIUM, 80s rock tribute band 8IGHTY 6IXX, and salsa band Calle Mambo. He lives in Massachusetts with his wonderful partner Kristen and the cutest nugget that ever nuggeted: Ollie!

Also Available From

HarmonyTabs

Sheet Music

-A Cappella Choirs/Groups
-Brass Ensembles
-String Ensembles
-Sax Ensembles
And More!

HARMONYTABS.COM/SHEET-MUSIC/

Songbooks

-Wind Ensembles
-A Cappella Choirs/Groups
-Flute Ensembles
-Brass Ensembles
And More!

HARMONYTABS.COM/MUSIC-BOOKS/SONGBOOKS/

Music Theory and Instruction

-An Incomplete Crash Course
in Contemporary Music Theory:
The Fundamentals

More to Come!

HARMONYTABS.COM/MUSIC-BOOKS/INSTRUCTIONAL-BOOKS/

Music Composition

-Standard Manuscript Notebook
-Pocket Manuscript Notebook
-Writing Prompt Journals

More to Come!

HARMONYTABS.COM/MUSIC-BOOKS/MUSIC-COMPOSITION-BOOKS/

HarmonyTabsMusic.com

www.ingramcontent.com/pod-product-compliance
Lightning Source LLC
Chambersburg PA
CBHW041124120626

46547CB00019B/2842

* 9 7 8 1 9 6 1 7 3 5 2 2 4 *